Animals
that Burrow

Words by Dean Morris

Raintree Childrens Books
Milwaukee • Toronto • Melbourne • London

Library of Congress Number: 77-8114

1 2 3 4 5 6 7 8 9 0 81 80 79 78 77

Printed and bound in the United States of America.

Library of Congress Cataloging in Publication Data

Morris, Dean.
    Animals that burrow.

    (Read about)
    Includes index.
    SUMMARY: An introduction to mammals, birds, insects,
shellfish, and other creatures that make their homes
underground.
    1. Burrowing animals — Juvenile literature.
[1. Burrowing animals] I. Title.
QL49.M798   591.5   77-8114
ISBN 0-8393-0012-3

This book has been reviewed
for accuracy by

Dr. Max Allen Nickerson
Head, Vertebrate Division
Milwaukee Public Museum

Animals
that Burrow

mole

bank
swallow

These animals are different in several ways. Some of them have fur. Some have feathers. Some have claws. Some have fins.

But these animals have one important thing in common.

These animals

ground squirrels

mole rat

usually live in holes that they dig themselves. Digging a hole in which to live is called burrowing.

In this book, you will learn about some of the animals that burrow. But first, let's look at *why* they do it.

earthworm

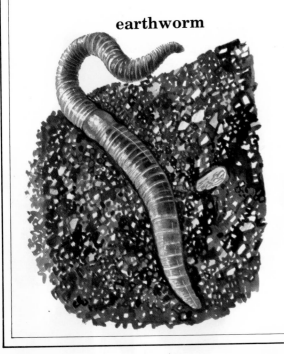

lungfish

lizard

rattlesnake

kangaroo rat

Some animals make burrows to protect themselves from the weather. In the desert where it is dry and hot, animals burrow to keep cool and save water.

Gila woodpecker

elf owl

desert tortoise

chuckwalla

Some desert animals dig holes in the big cactus plants. Others burrow into the ground. Lizards may hide under logs or rocks.

Most animals stay in their burrows during the hot part of the day. They come out at night and when the weather is cool.

Burrowing is one way that animals adapt to the place they live. Adapting means changing to stay alive.

Burrows protect animals from their enemies too. This snake slides into its burrow to get away from the hawk. Many animals burrow to hide from other animals that might eat them.

hawk

burrowing snake

armadillo

The armadillo's body is covered with armor. But its armor does not always keep it safe. When an armadillo is attacked, it often runs to a burrow.

Fairy armadillos are small animals. They live in underground burrows. Fairy armadillos have special plates at the end of their bodies. They may use the plates to block the doors of their burrows. Many enemies cannot get in.

ocelot

fairy armadillo

spiny anteater

Some animals can dig very fast. When the spiny anteater is disturbed, it digs with all four feet. It may raise its sharp "needles" as it digs. It may bury itself until only a small patch of "needles" is showing.

Animals sometimes burrow to get their food. Some woodpeckers eat insects called bark beetles. To get at the beetles, they peck holes in the trees. They often reach the beetles with their tongues.

Bark beetles burrow too. Female bark beetles make tunnels. They lay eggs one by one as they move along.

woodpecker

bark beetle
tunnels

Some burrows are good for storing food. Harvester ants collect seeds. They dig underground rooms in which to store the seeds. That way they can store food for the dry season when food is hard to find.

Sometimes animals take a rest from making burrows. In winter the ground may be cold and hard. Worms cannot move through hard, frozen soil. So they may "sleep" in a burrow until spring.

Small woodland animals such as skunks spend much of the winter in their burrows too. Skunks often line their burrows with leaves and grass.

Some animals may dig burrows to protect their young. Burrowing owls take over mammal and reptile burrows or they may even dig their own. They make nests in the holes. The baby owls stay in the burrows until they are old enough to get food for themselves.

burrowing owl

petrel

tuatara

Sometimes one kind of animal shares a burrow with another kind. Some petrels may dig burrows with their bills and feet.
They lay their eggs in the burrows. Tuataras live in some of the burrows with petrels. Sometimes a tuatara will eat a petrel egg.

Rabbits and puffins both make burrows. A puffin sometimes moves into a burrow left empty by a rabbit.

puffin

rabbit

These animals live on ocean beaches. They burrow into the sand and many birds and other animals cannot find them.

The lugworm lives in a burrow shaped like a U. It swallows sand along with small pieces of plants and animals. It pushes the sand out of its body and digests the plants and animals.

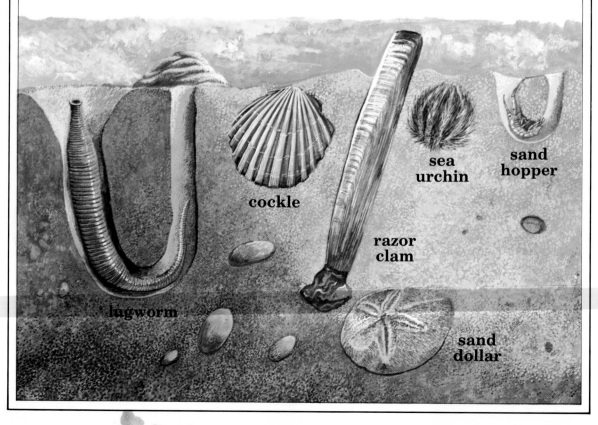

cockle

sea urchin

sand hopper

razor clam

lugworm

sand dollar

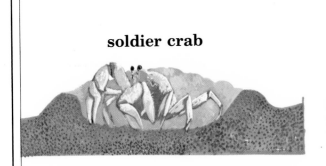

soldier crab

The soldier crab sometimes lives in muddy places near the sea. When the tide comes in, it often burrows into the sand. First it pushes up the wet sand until it is hidden. Then it digs deeper. It pats the sand in place, making a strong roof.

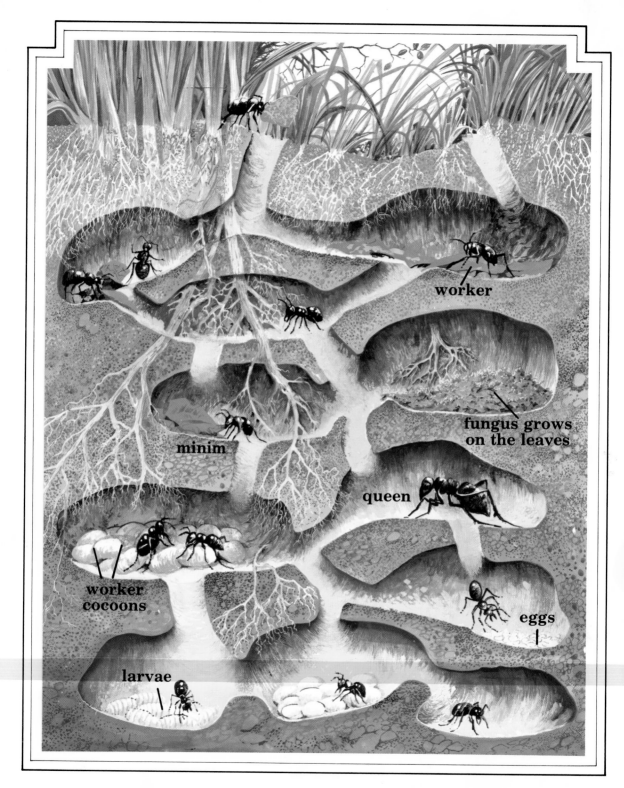

worker

fungus grows
on the leaves

minim

queen

eggs

worker
cocoons

larvae

Leaf-cutting ants sometimes live in nests underground. They dig many rooms in their nests. Some rooms are for eggs. The eggs hatch into larvae. The larvae are moved to other rooms. Some rooms are for storing food.

Each type of ant in the nest has its own job. Worker ants collect leaves and store them. Smaller workers, called minims, chew the leaves. Later, the ants eat the fungus that has grown on the leaves. A fungus is a plant that often lives on other plants and animals.

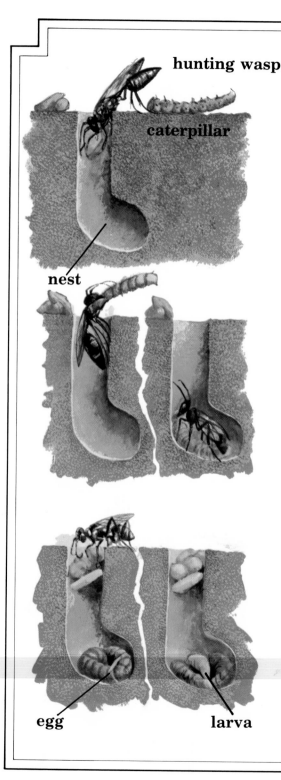

hunting wasp

caterpillar

nest

egg

larva

The hunting wasps are other insects that sometimes burrow. The female hunting wasp may dig holes in which to lay her eggs.

She often catches caterpillars and stings them so they cannot move. She puts one in each hole. Then she lays an egg on top of each caterpillar. She seals the burrow to hide the eggs.

Each egg hatches into a larva. The larvae suck the juices from the live caterpillars. The juices are their food.

Trap-door spiders may dig a burrow with the help of their "fangs." They line the inside of the hole with silk. The spider makes a trap door of silk and earth. Insects do not see the door. They get caught.

The spider stays inside the hole and holds onto the door. Many other animals cannot open the door to eat the spider.

trap-door spider

spadefoot toad

Spadefoot toads often live in hot, dry places, but they usually avoid the sun. They dig a hole with their horny back feet. They may "sleep" in this burrow until rain comes.

Many animals burrow along the banks of rivers and ponds. Pond turtles may make "burrows" before winter. They dig into the mud. The mud helps keep them warm.

pond turtles

water rat

Water voles,
water rats, and water
shrews all may make
their burrows along
river banks.

Some kingfishers
burrow with their
bills. They make
tunnels in the river
bank. They sometimes
make their nests at
the end of the tunnels.

kingfisher

water
vole

water
shrew

duck-billed platypus

The duck-billed platypus spends much of its time in the water, but its nest is underground. The platypus digs a burrow in the river bank. Sometimes the burrow has an underwater entrance. The platypus often lays its eggs at the end of the burrow. When the eggs hatch, the mother feeds her babies with her milk.

red fox

badgers

Some badgers live in the woods. They make several entrances to their burrows. During the day badgers may stay inside. They often come out at night to look for food.

Badgers collect plants to make beds in their burrows. They seem to be very clean animals. They usually change their bedding often.

Moles live underground most of their lives. They dig with their short, strong front paws. They loosen the soil by pushing their feet sideways. Some soil is pushed up. This often makes molehills on top of the ground wherever the mole has made a tunnel.

star-nosed mole

Some moles dig two kinds of burrows. Hunting burrows often run just under the ground. Moles move along them looking for food. Some moles' favorite foods are earthworms and insects.

hunting burrow

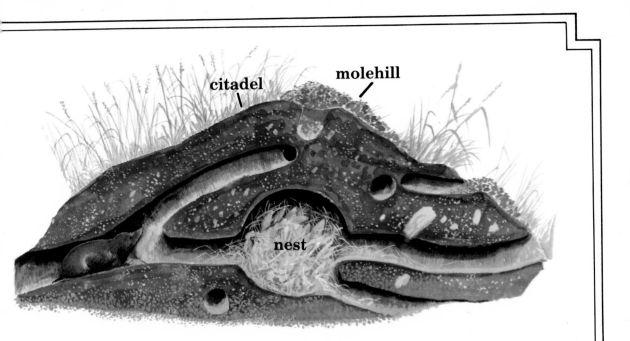

citadel

molehill

nest

A citadel is a burrow that a mole digs to live in. A citadel has tunnels which are all joined together. There is a nest in the "center." The nest is lined with grass and leaves.

Aardvarks are animals that live in Africa. They eat termites and some plants. An aardvark can dig a burrow very fast. When it is disturbed, it digs into the ground. It disappears in a few minutes. Aardvarks also dig burrows to live in. The burrows are large and neat. They have many tunnels and doors.

termite
nest

aardvarks

Wombats live in Australia. They dig burrows with many tunnels and rooms. Wombats often live near water. They often take baths.

A baby wombat rides in its mother's pouch. The baby often faces backward. When the mother digs, dirt does not get into the baby's face.

pouch

wombat

Pocket gophers may live alone in their burrows. The burrow has rooms for nesting, for storing food, and for wastes. The gopher often makes tunnels just below the ground. That is where it finds the plant stems it likes to eat.

nest

food store

Vizcachas live in South America. They live in groups of tunnels. They carry soil up from the tunnels and make high mounds. Vizcachas come out at night to hunt and collect things. They keep bones, stones, sticks, and other things they collect near their burrows.

vizcacha

Many animals make big burrows. But the prairie dogs may make the most extensive ones. Prairie dogs often live in huge underground towns. Hundreds and thousands of burrows may be connected by tunnels. Each prairie dog family has its own burrow.

Prairie dogs protect each other. They take turns standing guard at the entrances to the burrows. If a prairie dog guard sees a coyote or another enemy, it barks. The other prairie dogs run and hide. Prairie dogs sometimes share their burrows with rabbits, owls, and snakes.

coyote

prairie dogs

Where to Read About
Animals that Burrow

leaf-cutting ant (lēf′ kut′ ing   ant)
   pp. 18-19
lizard (liz′ ərd) *p. 7*
lugworm (lug′ wurm′) *p. 16*
lungfish (lung′ fish′) *p. 5*
mole (mōl) *pp. 4, 26-27*
mole rat (mōl   rat) *p. 5*
owl (oul) *p. 33*
petrel (pe′ trəl) *p. 15*
pocket gopher (pok′ it   gō′ fər) *p. 30*
pond turtle (pond   turt′ əl) *p. 22*
prairie dog (prer′ ē   dog) *pp. 32-33*
puffin (puf′ in) *p. 15*
rabbit (rab′ it) *pp. 15, 33*
rattlesnake (rat′ əl snāk′) *p. 6*
razor clam (rā′ zər   klam) *p. 16*
sand dollar (sand   dol′ ər) *p. 16*
sand hopper (sand   hop′ ər) *p. 16*
sea urchin (sē   ər′ chən) *p. 16*
skunk (skungk) *p. 13*
snake (snāk) *pp. 8, 33*
soldier crab (sōl′ jər   krab) *p. 17*

Pronunciation Key for Glossary

a	a as in **cat, bad**
ā	a as in **able,** ai as in **train,** ay as in **play**
ä	a as in **father, car**
e	e as in **bend, yet**
ē	e as in **me,** ee as in **feel,** ea as in **beat,** ie as in **piece,** y as in **heavy**
i	i as in **in, pig**
ī	i as in **ice, time,** ie as in **tie,** y as in **my**
o	o as in **top**
ō	o as in **old,** oa as in **goat,** ow as in **slow,** oe as in **toe**
ô	o as in **cloth,** au as in **caught,** aw as in **paw,** a as in **all**
oo	oo as in **good,** u as in **put**
o͞o	oo as in **tool,** ue as in **blue**
oi	oi as in **oil,** oy as in **toy**
ou	ou as in **out,** ow as in **plow**
u	u as in **up, gun,** o as in **other**
ur	ur as in **fur,** er as in **person,** ir as in **bird,** or as in **work**
yo͞o	u as in **use,** ew as in **few**
ə	a as in **again,** e as in **broken,** i as in **pencil,** o as in **attention,** u as in **surprise**
ch	ch as in **such**
ng	ng as in **sing**
sh	sh as in **shell, wish**
th	th as in **three, bath**
<u>th</u>	th as in **that, together**

GLOSSARY

These words are defined the way they are used in this book.

adapt (ə dapt′) to change to fit
new conditions

alive (ə līve′) living; not dead; having life

armor (är′ mər) a covering that protects the
body of a person or an animal

attack (ə tak′) begin to fight against
an enemy

avoid (ə void′) to stay away from

backward (bak′ wərd) away from; toward
the back

beach (bēch) sandy or stony land at the edge
of an ocean or lake

beetle (bēt′ əl) an insect with two pairs
of wings, one of which acts as a hard
protective cover

bill (bil) a bird's hard mouthpart

body (bod′ ē) the whole of a person,
animal, or plant

bone (bōn) a hard, stiff part of the skeleton

of most animals with backbones

burrow (bur′ ō) a hole in the ground or in something else that is used as a nest by some animals and insects

burrowing (bur′ ō ing) digging into the ground or into something else in order to make a home

bury (ber′ ē) to put something into a hole and cover it

cactus (kak′ təs) a plant often found in the desert that has a thick stem and spines instead of leaves

cannot (kan′ ot *or* ka not′) is not able; can not

caterpillar (kat′ ər pil′ ər) the wormlike larva of a butterfly or moth

center (sen′ tər) the middle point or part of a thing

chew (choo) to use teeth or jaws to grind up food or something else

citadel (sit′ əd əl′ *or* sit′ ə del′) a kind of burrow made by a mole

claw (klô) a type of nail, often sharp and

curved, found on an animal's foot

collect (kə lekt') to bring several things together

common (kom' ən) usual; something that happens often; the same for all

connect (kə nekt') to join or fasten together

cool (ko͞ol) rather cold; not warm

coyote (kī ō' tē *or* kī' ōt) an animal that looks like a wolf

desert (dez' ərt) a dry, often hot place where few plants grow

digest (di jest' *or* dī jest') to change food inside the body into a form that the body can use

dirt (durt) loose earth, mud, or dust

disturb (dis turb') made uneasy; moved from its usual place

earthworm (urth' wurm') a long-bodied worm that lives in soil

entrance (en' trəns) a place through which someone or something can get in

extensive (eks ten' siv) large; broad in range

fang (fang) a long tooth that is pointed
at the end

favorite (fā' vər it) best liked

female (fē' māl) of the sex that has babies
or produces eggs

fin (fin) a thin, movable part of a fish's
body that sticks out and is used to swim
and to keep balance in the water

frozen (frō' zən) made hard when the air
around something is very cold

fungus (fung' gəs) a plant without leaves or
stems that lives and grows on other plants,
animals, and soil

grown (grōn) lived; existed; become as large
as it is supposed to become

hatch (hach) to come from inside an egg

hawk (hôk) a bird that attacks other living
things for its food

hidden (hid' ən) put in a place where
something cannot be seen or
easily found

horny (hôr' nē) made of a hard,
tough material

huge (hyo͞oj) very large

insect (in′ sekt) a small animal, often with a hard outer covering, without a backbone, such as a fly or ant

itself (it self′) that same one

juice (jo͞os) the liquid from fruits, vegetables, and meats

larva (lär′ və) the wormlike form of an insect after it hatches from an egg
plural **larvae**

larvae see **larva**

log (lôg *or* log) a piece of the trunk or a branch of a tree, cut at each end, with the bark still on

loosen (lo͞o′ sən) to make something less tight or able to move more freely

mammal (mam′ əl) a warm-blooded animal with a backbone and often with a growth of hair or fur

minim (min′ əm) a small worker ant that chews leaves on which fungus grows for ants' food

molehill (mōl′ hil) a mound of earth formed

when moles dig tunnels

mound (mound) a small hill made of piled
up earth, stones, or other material

ocelot (os′ ə lot′ *or* ō′ sə lot′) a wildcat
that has a yellowish coat marked by
black stripes, rings and spots

patch (pach) a small piece of something

peck (pek) to make a short, quick movement
with the bill

plate (plāt) a hard, flat covering that helps
protect an animal

pouch (pouch) a baglike part of some female
animals used to carry their young

reptile (rep′ təl *or* rep′ tīl) a cold-
blooded animal with a backbone and dry,
scaly skin

seal (sēl) to close something tightly

season (sē′ zən) any part of the year that has
a certain kind of weather, such as rainy or dry

share (sher) to use with others; to give to
someone else part of what one has

sideways (sīd′ wāz′) a movement to or from
one side

silk (silk) soft, shiny threads made by some insects

soil (soil) the soft, top part of the ground; earth

spider (spī′ dər) a small, wingless animal with four pairs of legs and a body divided into two parts that spins a web to trap insects for its food

stem (stem) the main part of a plant from which leaves and flowers grow

sting (sting) a wound made by an insect; to wound with a sharp point

suck (suk) to draw something into the mouth

swallow (swol′ ō) to take food in through the mouth and pass it into the stomach

termite (tur′ mīt) an insect that lives with others like itself in a large group and often eats wood and paper

themselves (them selvz′ *or* thəm selvz′) the same ones

thousand (thou′ zənd) the number 1,000

tide (tīd) the movement of oceans and other large bodies of water that causes a rise and fall about every twelve hours

tongue (tung) a movable part of the mouth
used for tasting and swallowing

tunnel (tun′ əl) an underground or
underwater passage

type (tīp) a kind or group of things that are
alike in some ways

underground (un′ dər ground′) a place below
the surface of the earth

woodland (wood′ lənd) land that is covered
with trees and other plants

Bibliography

Burton, Maurice, and Burton, Robert, editors.
The International Wildlife Encyclopedia.
20 vols. Milwaukee: Purnell Reference
Books, 1970.

Davis, Bette J. *Mole from the Meadow.*
New York: Lathrop, Lee & Shepard Company,
1970.
Observations on the habits and behavior
of the common mole as well as its molehills,
ancestors, and other creatures in its
environment.

Fisher, Aileen Lucia. *Valley of the Smallest:
The Life Story of a Shrew.* New York:
Thomas Y. Crowell, 1966.

Laycock, George. *Squirrels.* New York:
Four Winds Press, 1975.
Discusses the characteristics and
behavior of and many little-known
facts about squirrels and such
cousins of theirs as the chipmunk,
woodchuck, sik-sik, and prairie dog.

May, Julian. *Life Cycle of a Fox.*
Chicago: Childrens Press, 1973.